Life Is For Living

Donna Bloedow

BookLeaf Publishing

Presentation by *BookLeaf Publishing*

Web: www.bookleafpub.com

E-mail: info@bookleafpub.com

ISBN: 9789358736663

First edition 2023

Someone

Someone to sit and converse quietly with
Someone who truly does care
Someone who shows by word and deed
When called upon, you'll be there.

Someone I confide in when I'm troubled
Someone I tell my good news
Someone who shares advice with me
But will still respect my views.

Someone i trust with all my heart
Someone with whom I'm secure
Someone who always stands by me
Who's actions toward me are pure.

Someone I turn to in times of need
Someone who turns to me
Someone with whom I can be myself
Wherever we happen to be.

You are my Special Someone.

Walking On The Beach

It's a wonderful time to be here
The sun now going to rest
I believe this time of the evening
Must surely be the best.

I stand at the water's edge
Soft sand caressing my feet
My toes reach to feel the water
Relief from the day's searing heat.

Walking along in the shallows
I place each foot with care
Not willing to miss the beauty
Which I always find is there.

A walk with no purpose, no meaning
A walk with no end; with no start
A walk in the cool summer evening
A walk that renews my heart.

The daylight is swiftly fading
It heralds the coming of night
I gaze o'er the azure blue water
It is truly a wonderful sight.

As small waves lap at my ankles
And sand slides under my feet
As the cool breeze caresses my shoulders
I am thankful for summer heat.

It makes the beach so welcoming
Summoning the youth in me
Time seems to stand quietly still
Things feel just as they used to be.

Why must it all end, just when it feels the best?

Seven Five Three One

Seeing, knowing, watching all
Mirror to the soul
Observant
Eyes.

Making sense from jumbled noise
Listening to sounds
Hearing things
Ears.

Sniff, smell, send message to brain
Sneeze, sniffle, dripping,
Wrinkle, sting
Nose.

Communicate emotions
Make sounds, speak, whistle
Taste, change shape
Mouth.

Interpreting everything
Logical sorting
Making sense
Mind.

Long, round, square, oval, large, small
Pretty, plain, homely
Show feelings
Face.

Emotions, needs, likes, dislikes
Personality
Unique gifts
Self.

Death Of An Island

All day long the sun shines bright
The moon shines high all through the night
The children sleep, their parents talk
Somewhere, someone has gone to stalk.

At break of day the sun shines proud
The sky is clear, no sign of a cloud
But no birds sing though the sun is high
By noon there's grey clouds in the sky.

A storm is coming in from the sea
when it passes this island it will carry me
Many a cyclone, many a storm
Have passed this island yet left us alone.

But this one I know will carry me away
Today on this earth shall be my last day.
I feel it in my blood, my bones
My time has come to leave this earthly home.

Think of me always oh people of mine
For this is only a warning sign
A cyclone will follow with it you'll all go
But in the Spirit World together we'll roam.

*written when I was twelve.

My Time To Shine

There is a sea of candles,
Each one shining bright
Lighting up the darkness
But where is my light

Like a tiny candle
Flickering and dim
Been alone too long
Been out on a limb

Now it's my time to shine
Yes it's my time to shine
My time to shine
Oh it's my time to shine.

So bring your candle closer
Let's hold our light up high
We'll break through the darkness
Together we can fly

Many tiny candles
With small unshaken flame
All held up high together
As one voice we exclaim

Now it's my time to shine
Yes it's my time to shine
My time to shine
Oh it's my time to shine.

Oh it's my time to shine
To shine forever more.

It's A Dog's Year

January is thick with humidity, as you paddle in
the ocean.

February is perfect for car rides, with your head
out the window, tongue lolling.

In March the sun shines brightly, as I watch you
digging in the sand. Head down, bum up, tail
wagging.

April bring rain showers, to rejuvenate the
gardens; and us. You splatter through puddles
and bring mud into the house.

May is the perfect time for barbeques and
picnics; for sniffing and exploring.

June brings cooler winds, and days that are
shorter, for walks in the park, and early bed
times.

July has a bite in the air, we don't venture out
for too long, though you still patrol your
territory and ward off strangers.

August is a month of contrasts. Swim one day, huddle by the heater, the next. Always watchful, alert and ready for a game.

In September the harsh winds have gone and the sun smiles down once more. You have a spring in your step and a stick in your mouth.

October is perfect for ferry rides and exploring the waterways, for splashing about and shaking yourself dry.

November bring smells from the deep blue yonder, closer to the shoreline; to tantalise and tease your nostrils.

December is the time for chasing birds at the park, watching them rise up and soar away to safety. Your face has a smile as your eyes follow them.

Life's Road

Sometimes the road seems too long
And I'm travelling far too fast
I yearn to slow down for a while
And watch the other go past.

Just for a while and then
I'll journey on some more
But for a while I need to rest
I am weary and footsore.

But if I stop I fear
I'll like the resting so much
I won't want to go any further
And road's end I never will touch.

So I realise I must try harder
Detour not by the way
I must be ready when Christ comes
And that could be any day.

The shadows are growing longer
The evening is coming on
And if I am not mindful
The chance to repent will be gone.

Then it will be too late
To travel along the road
So I must not stop and rest
I must carry on with my load.

The Saviour my burdens will bear.

Autumn Morning

When I arise in the morning
The horizon starts to grow light
It cheers up the trees and the bushes
As they slowly awake from the night.

The earth is so still, so quiet
Then one by one the birds rise
They sing their songs of glory
As they willingly take to the skies.

This peaceful scene before me
Helps me feel joyful and new
The scented flowers are lovely
Petals glisten with dew.

A car starts up in the distance
A light goes on over the way
I smile my heartfelt gratitude
At the start of this brand new day.

The sun is climbing higher now
Daylight shines in full force
The sun's rays stretch endlessly
Nature's beauty they endorse.

On such a morning as this
I prayerfully ponder, reflect
At the wonder of God who created it
I sit here and gaze in respect.

Words Of Wisdom (or something…)

If you steal ---
Steal time for your self.

If you cheat ---
Cheat death.

If you lie ---
Lie with the one you love (I suggest a dog or a
teddy bear).

If you drink ---
Drink to the good health of all you meet (I
would choose something non alcoholic).

If you judge —-
Judge righteously and with compassion.

If you look down —-
Look down to help somebody up.

If you fall —-
Fall deeply
Fall madly
In love.

Hiding Behind The Law

You call it law, you say it helps
To keep all safe and yet
Who saves the chosen ones
From your law, from your mates?

Why will nobody listen
Nor hear the plaintive cries
Why is there no one to turn to
Who won't dismiss it as lies?

Who will pick up the pieces
And mend the broken hearts
None; all are absolved
Once they've fulfilled their parts.

Only harken to the preacher man
Never heed the ragged crone
He speaks for all, yea speaks it well.
Though his heart be made of stone.

Lonely cries are hushed and quieted
Lest some should seek to find
The truth that's long been hidden
Inside the pauper's mind.

You call it law and hide behind
The words that are blood red
You stamp your gavel, it is done
There's naught more to be said.

No one bares the guilt of blame. It was the law
who spoke.

Why Do We Suffer

Suffering is human
It lets us know we live
It says with clear expression
That we have more to give.

Through exquisite suffering
We reach out and we yearn
For our suffering to be ended
For the lesson to be learned.

Through suffering we learn
That we truly can endure
We also learn compassion
As we pray for a cure.

Suffering helps remind us
Of times we've felt so free
When pain was so far from us
We thought 't'would always be.

We bend to lift another
Whose burdens we can share
For suffering has taught us
That our joy, we need to share.

When we've suffered exquisitely
When we thought we could not endure
We turn to our Heavenly Father
For His blessings pure.

We would not wish this suffering
On another living soul
We seek from deep within us
For our selves to be made whole.

Suffering does bind us
To others we may meet
So we can ease their burdens
As each other we kindly greet.

Scintillating Scent Of Silent Soul

Silence overwhelms my soul
At dusk and in the darkened night
Thoughts creep in and steal away
The peaceful bliss of slumber.

Steady streams of breath float by
An unforgotten scent
Lingers o'er my *nasus*
Where I reach, to ease my longing.

Sweet smell that is my talisman
Trailing long after life has passed
Filtering through the cold, harsh atmosphere
Of forgotten dreams and shattered hopes.

Memories remain, long since that scent has vanished.

Life's Mission

Each morn I wake to face the day
I thank Thee, my Father in Heaven
That Thou art with me, thus I pray
Please make me fit for Heaven.

Help me be more positive
When I feel deep despair
When times are tough, I need to know
That Thou art always there.

When I feel far off from Thee
'T'is my own fault, I know
For Christ hath clearly marked the path
Showing the way to go.

Veiled in the flesh, Thy face I seek
To guide my mortal feet
The upward, onward way to Thee
When my time on Earth is complete.

In times when trials seem so tough
When life feels so unfair
Help me seek the wandering soul
Whose burdens I can share.

Thus would I be doing Thy will
Life's mission be in plain view
To bring souls unto Christ the Lord
Premortal covenants renew.

Thou sent us here to do a work
The plan is set before us
Help me to fulfil my task
Then join that Heavenly chorus.

Singing Hallelujahs
Ever to Thy Holy name
World, after world, endless
Hallelujahs, all the same.

My Earthly mission is not done yet.

Toddlers

Muddy footprints on the floor
Fingerprints upon the wall
Sticky patches underfoot
Crayon scribbles in the hall.

Taps left dripping in the bathroom
Toys lying on the old armchair
Uneaten vegies on the table
Sure signs a toddler's living there.

Loud wailing, running feet
Sticky face, a grimy hand
Grubby shirt and trousers too
Eyes shut tight, filled with sand.

Trusting mum to clean his eyes
Fill his tummy and soothe his hurt
Pick up his toys, turn off the tap
Help him find a clean, dry shirt.

Day is never long enough
To finish all the household chores
Seems his nap has just begun
When out he comes slamming doors.

Mum wonders why she bothers each day
With such a noisy, messy lad
Then he gives a hug and kiss
It's now the best day she's ever had.

She has forgotten how to be house proud.

Colours

25

The sand whips across the shore
Like a sprinkling of sharp yellow glass.

The singing sea has a melody of blue
That tickles my senses and lifts my spirit.

The dancing towel glitters like rich red rubies
As it pirouettes playfully with the joyful breeze.

Like a huge woollen blanket of shimmering
green
The hill wrapped in warmth beckons to my feet.

Maths

Numbers everywhere I go
Fractions, decimals, metric too
Numbers for a recipe, numbers for the phone
Numbers for every little thing that I do.

Numbers on a street map
Numbers at the shop
Prices in the supermarket
Where does maths stop?

Geometry and algebra
Those X and A and Cs
To some it's so confusing
Yet some can do it with ease.

I have a calculator
To think my maths for me
It makes it very easy - but
Where can the darned thing be?

I've hunted high and low for it
I've searched both here and there
I'm really lost without it
Oh it just isn't fair!

How can I do my budget
How can I add my bills
I stood and used my fingers
I did look such a dill.

I wish I had have listened
To my teacher in high school
Then I wouldn't be counting
Out loud like a bloody fool.

I'd know how long a furlong is
I'd know how to use pi
I'd understand angles and quarters
And the dreaded X and Y.

So while you have the chance
Please learn your maths well
So you don't rely on a calculator
That's lost and gone to hell!

While Roses Have Colour

I am the wind that whistles past
I am the thick strong Guinea grass
I am in the trees that sway
I am the sand upon the bay.

I am the ocean waves so wild
I am the one who's an endless child
I am the stones on a craggy shore
I am all this and so much more.

I can never be tamed by man nor beast
I can never be stilled, nay not in the least
I am a spirit and have no need of wings
I am in the gentle breeze that sings.

I will always be present while roses have colour.

My Confidant

He sits with hazel eyed gaze
A Mona Lisa smile plays on his lips
Still as a statue he sits in one place
When I speak ne'er a word he quips.

He listens so intently
I can tell by his rapt attention
So encouraged I share all my views
Though to confide was not my intention.

Still on and on as I ramble
He sits there and listens to me
As I confide, my heart grows lighter
Everyone needs a friend such as he.

His eyes so bright and so caring
Gaze intently upon my wet cheek
I know as I talk he is feeling
The sorrow of which I can't speak.

Still, as I watch his soulful eyes
And see no judgement there
I speak and although but a whisper
He sees and somehow shows he cares.

I tell him my innermost secrets
Things no one else knows about me
I trust him he never betrays
The things he hears and sees.

No movement he makes to disturb
The reverie which we both feel
As I finally stop talking and crying
The peace in me is so real.

Yes this friend so tender and loving
With a warm and huggable embrace
Is my very special confidant
I can see it in his soft loving face.

Ah how I love my teddy bear.

The Beauty Of A Rose

I think of a beautiful rose
In shades of pink of red
I marvel at how it grows
In a neglected garden bed.

I gently pluck the blossom
Taking care for surrounding thorns
Such danger masked by beauty
Much like Joshua's horns.

Soft petals I gently caress
Sweet peacefulness fills my soul
Each petal a perfect piece
Formed to make a whole.

The intricacy of the rose
The allurement of it's sight
The pleasant summer fragrance
That is barely dimmed by night.

Oh that I could reach my potential
And see my own self worth
For like each shade of rose
I've been made royal - by birth.

May my fragrance outweigh my thorns.

Alphabet Owl's View

Amongst the mess I sit and stare
But you don't seem to know I'm there
Carefree into your cupboard you squeeze
Doubled over at the knees.

Enough already! I'll be sick!
Fully bare as clothes you pick.
Goodness no wonder my eyes are wide
Helpless from such a view to hide.

Ignorant to the scene you pose
Jutting out amid your clothes
Kung fu fighting into a shirt
Lungs contract as you try on a skirt.

Make another choice or two
Nothing seems to fit on you
Owls, we just grow larger feathers
Protected in all kinds of weathers.

Quietly I laugh Too-Whit Too-Whoo.

God's Special Child

I'm sending you for just a while
This special child. God whispered
I know you'll give her all your love
Though the future to you may seem blurred.

I have sought throughout the world
For the special parent who
Would be the best one for this child
That's how I selected you.

She may need care for many years
Or only just a few
One day I'll take her back again
Until then she's entrusted to you.

She may not look like other girls
She may lower her head to walk
She'll often retreat to her own silent world
She may not fluently talk.

But she will feel the love you have
Although it may not show
She needs much help and strength from you
For she has far to go.

She will love you, in her heart
She will rely on you
To advocate the best for her
It will often be just you two.

Others may not understand
Their judgement can be cruel
Working with specialists may be a trial
As will be finding just the right school.

At times it may seem too difficult
And you'll wonder if you'll get through
But please remember, mum of this child
That I will be there for you.

I listened and I'm pleased I heard
"Dear Lord be it unto me."
You'll brave the challenges ahead
You'll return this child safely to me.

You'll tenderly care for all her needs
You'll guide her toward My light
Please remember, when you need me,
I'll be never far from sight.

"Dear Lord I will rely on You
To hear my pleas for help and care
I know I can not do it alone
Thy child with Thee, I'll share.

I will read all the books I can
To learn about her needs
I'll try but few to understand
Where her disability leads.

I somehow feel, Dear Lord,
As though I already understand
It seems that I know this path
We are walking hand in hand."

I know you understand — you have her needs
too.